101

Helpful Hints for Backcountry
and Pleasure Riding

TRAIL RIDING TIPS

Dan Aadland

The Lyons Press
Guilford, Connecticut
An imprint of The Globe Pequot Press

The Lyons Press is an imprint of The Globe Pequot Press

10 9 8 7 6 5 4 3 2 1

Printed in the United States of America

Designed by Sheryl P. Kober

Library of Congress Cataloging-in-Publication Data

Aadland, Dan.
   101 trail riding tips : helpful hints for backcountry and pleasure riding / by Dan Aadland.
        p. cm.
   ISBN 1-59228-830-8 (trade paper)
   1. Trail riding. I. Title. II. Title: One hundred one trail riding tips.
   SF309.28.A226 2005
   798.2′3—dc22

                                   2005023621

101

TRAIL RIDING TIPS

Also by Dan Aadland

Treading Lightly with Pack Animals

Women and Warriors of the Plains

Horseback Adventures

Sketches from the Ranch: A Montana Memoir

The Complete Trail Horse: Selecting, Training, and Enjoying Your Horse in the Backcountry

Contents

Introduction

Many centuries ago, according to the poet Geoffrey Chaucer, twenty-nine people sat on horses that chewed their bits and pawed the ground in their impatience to hit the trail. In the party were a knight on his charger, a chase-loving monk on his hunter, and the Wife of Bath on her smooth-traveling ambler. The avowed purpose of these riders was a pilgrimage to Canterbury, England, to commemorate the death of religious martyr Thomas a' Becket, but there was nothing sorrowful in their demeanor. Adventure they were after, wrote the poet, and fellowship with all. The atmosphere was festive, the riders relishing the horseback journey ahead of them.

Equestrians have changed little since Chaucer's time. Many horseback activities are engaging. Showing, eventing, jumping, racing, cutting, and reining all have appeal. Yet the simple act of covering ground, new ground if possible, on the back of a good saddle horse must be the most alluring of all, for trail and pleasure riding are America's number one horse activity. Like the pilgrims heading to Canterbury, we assemble at trailheads, tack up our horses while chattering with kindred spirits, then head out with eyes wide and ears at the ready. Our mode of travel allows interaction with nature unadulterated by the smelly cacophony of internal combustion engines. We hear the trickling brook, the songbirds, the bugle of an elk. The sound of hoofbeats and the occasional whinny of a horse complement the scene instead of destroying it.

This book is intended as a quick reference to help with horsemanship outside the arena—with attention paid to your safety, your horse's safety, and the care of the land. I'll be thankful for anything this book does to sustain in you the spirit of those riders who traveled to Canterbury seven hundred years ago.

Chapter 1

Safety

Our series of tips begins with safety. Trail riding is not particularly dangerous—but whenever you're dealing with large, powerful animals and rough terrain, the potential for serious accidents certainly exists. In this chapter we'll focus on how to interact safely with horses. In later chapters, we'll furnish tips on coping with hazards in the environment.

Horses are domestic herd animals.

tip 1. Understand the nature of horses

Understanding the horse's nature is your first line of defense for safe interaction with an animal many times your own size, weight, and strength. Horses are wonderful creatures, beautiful to look at, satisfying to touch, rewarding to know. They are also fully capable of hurting or even killing you. The good news is that all horses are domestic animals—not wild—and they carry in their genes a certain simpatico with humans, just as dogs do. The other side of the coin is that they're herd animals with deeply ingrained survival instincts. These instincts, if not understood and shaped by training, can be dangerous.

A horse's first impulse when confronted with anything it believes to be potentially dangerous is to flee. If escape is impossible, its alternative reaction is to fight—either by whirling and kicking with its hind feet or by biting and striking with its front feet. Safe interaction with horses begins with remembering that these survival instincts remain intact even in the gentlest, best-trained horses.

Travis is relaxed, but he's also ready—necessary qualities on even the gentlest horse.

tip 2. Be relaxed but ready

Safety with horses begins by not holding them to higher standards than you would hold another human. Therefore, do not add the word *proof* to horses—as in childproof, spookproof, or bombproof. We don't consider ourselves infallible, incapable of making an unexplainable mistake. The best-trained, gentlest horse might also forget his training because of a sudden fright, a bee sting, or a strange smell or noise that humans, with weaker senses, don't perceive. The best attitude around horses is that of relaxed readiness. The relaxation is contagious; your horse will tend to relax as well. But keep in the back of your mind that with horses, things can change quickly. Handle them in ways that minimize danger, should the horse react to an unexpected stimulus.

It's always safest to approach at the shoulder.

tip 3. Approach at the shoulder

Humans, cats, and dogs developed as predators, but horses were primarily prey and thus have a different sort of vision. Predators look directly at things; prey animals constantly scan wide sweeps around them. Horses have nearly 360-degree vision, with a small blind area a few feet directly in front of them and a similar blind area behind. Too often humans make the mistake of treating their horses exactly as they would their pet cats or dogs, heading directly toward their faces from the front. Horses can find such an approach intimidating. They're far more comfortable with you at their side, approximately at the shoulder. They can see you perfectly well in that position and you, in turn, are more protected from the dangerous portions of a horse's anatomy: its rear feet, front feet, and teeth.

Particularly with horses you do not know, approach from the side at the shoulder, reaching out gently and touching the withers, then stroking them, something most horses enjoy. Your position at the side also allows you to move with the horse. In case of a spook, you are far safer there than being in front of him.

Halter at the shoulder, dropping the halter over the neck, then raising it into place.

tip 4. Halter your horse safely

Haltering a horse is most safely done from the side, not the front. Do not approach your horse directly from the front and attempt to place the halter on his face. Instead, grasp only the top strap of an opened halter. Standing at the base of the horse's neck on his left (near) side, reach over the top of his neck with the halter in hand and drop all but the top strap, which you retain in your hand. The halter now hangs in a convenient position over the horse's neck, and most horses believe they are "caught" at this point. Now slide the halter forward until it hangs below his chin and use your left hand to position and steady the halter. As you raise your right hand, pull the halter gently over the horse's nose where you can secure it with the top strap, using either a buckle or, with a rope halter, the correct knot.

A horse should be taught to lead with a loose rope by a handler walking at the base of his neck.

tip 5. Lead at the base of the neck

Because a position off the shoulder or slightly forward of that is the *safe zone*, that's also the traditional position from which horses are taught to lead. The well-schooled horse walks alongside you in that position with slack in the lead rope. If you lead from in front of your horse, your back is toward him. Should the animal spook, he might jump into you.

However, trail horses need to be taught to lead quietly behind you when walking down a narrow or tree-lined trail on which there is not room for the two of you side by side. Any well-mannered horse will respect your space, so walk in front in such restricted areas—nudging the horse's chest with your elbow or tapping with the lead rope to make him understand that in this particular location you want him behind you.

Pass behind closely with an arm on his rump, or stay far back out of kicking range.

tip 6. Pass behind a horse carefully

Passing behind a horse can be done in two ways. The safest is to pass well back behind the range of a possible kick, while talking to the horse to let him know you are there. With horses you trust, pass very close, keeping your hand on the horse's rump, again while talking to him. The worst distance at which to pass behind a horse is several feet; a kick at that range is the most destructive.

The horse will be more comfortable if you're both on one side.

tip 7. Work on one side

When helping another person work on a horse—whether grooming, administering medication, or trimming feet—it's safest if both of you work on the same side. As we've said, with horses surprise tends to be followed instantly by an attempt to escape. With a trained horse tied to a hitching rail, this may only involve a sudden step to one side, but even that can cause injury should the horse step on you or push you aside. Because horses are claustrophobic and need their space, they're less intimidated by two people on one side of them than by one on each side. The horse will be more relaxed and you'll both be safer if you both work on one side, allowing the horse some "escape space" should something startle him.

This horse is properly tied.

tip 8. Tie high and short

Tie a horse at his natural nose level or higher with approximately 1 1/2 to 2 feet of slack lead rope. Tying lower with too much slack encourages a horse to step over the lead rope and become entangled. If a horse is tied relatively high, he cannot pull back nearly as hard and is thus less likely to break a lead rope, the snap, or a hitching rail—possibly injuring himself or someone behind him.

A boot with the toe designed to find the stirrup, uppers to protect, slick sole to prevent getting caught, and heel to guard against going through the stirrup.

tip 9. **Wear boots**

Riding boots are more than a fashion statement. They're designed to protect you in several ways. The uppers are high enough to protect your ankle and calf from chafing against the stirrup and stirrup leathers. The soles are slick, not traction tread, to minimize the chance of hanging up in the stirrup while you dismount. The prominent heels help prevent your foot from sliding through the stirrup in case of a mishap, thus helping avoid one of the most terrible riding accidents: being thrown, hanging up, and then being dragged. For safety, don't wear sneakers, flip-flops, or sandals while riding.

Wearing a helmet is always wise.

tip 10. Wear a helmet

Most catastrophic injuries involve head trauma, so the wisdom of wearing a helmet is a no-brainer (if you can excuse the pun). Helmets have improved over the years—not only in ability to protect, but in comfort as well. That said, culture is a strong thing, and many of us gravitate toward headgear we consider more comfortable and more protective from rain, snow, sleet, and sun. If that's your orientation, make a concession and wear a helmet when working with a green horse, when riding vigorously, and, of course, any time a child rider is involved.

tip 11. Dress right

Dress appropriately for riding. Protecting your legs from chafe against the saddle leathers requires trousers, not shorts. Avoid loose, floppy garments—anything that could snag on the saddle horn (if you ride Western) during mounting or dismounting. In forested areas where you tend to rub against branches on narrow portions of the trail, long-sleeved shirts furnish more protection than short-sleeved ones. Your hat (if you haven't chosen to wear a helmet) should have enough brim to protect your face and neck from the sun. If it's rain resistant, so much the better.

tip 12. Fasten the main cinch first and remove it last

If your saddle has attachments such as a breast collar, a rear cinch, or a crupper, remember a simple rule for saddling and unsaddling: the main cinch always goes on first and comes off last. That way the saddle, which is held primarily by the main cinch, is always either secure or not attached at all. Should you fasten the breast collar first and a sudden spook occurs, the saddle could be half-attached—not free to come off entirely but not held securely either. At the very least, a saddle hanging under a horse's belly is likely to be ruined by the resulting wreck.

A good, rugged tapadero.

tip 13. Add tapaderos

Valued by the cavalrymen and vaqueros of the past and still standard equipment for field trial aficionados who follow their dogs through brush and bramble, tapaderos are all too neglected by today's trail riders. "Taps" protect your feet from rain and snow and prevent their being snagged and scratched by branches. More important, tapaderos prevent that horrifying accident of a foot slipping all the way through the stirrup and the rider being dragged after a fall.

Tapaderos with oversized stirrups allow you to wear bulky cold weather boots during winter. They'll protect your feet from splash when you ford a stream and your exuberant horse makes things worse by pawing the water. Extremely valuable for all riders, tapaderos should be mandatory equipment on any child's saddle.

tip 14. Avoid loops (and the reason split reins are safer)

Avoid loops of all kinds hanging off the saddle of your horse. If you carry a lead rope tied to the saddle strings, coil it tightly. Anything dangling in the form of a loop has the potential to snag an arm or leg, should you fall or be thrown or even when you are mounting or dismounting. For this reason split (two-piece) reins, which are safer than a single (one-piece, loop-type) rein, should be the eventual equipment for the finished backcountry horse.

tip 15. Warm up your horse

Before mounting a horse, warm him up. Lunging or warm-up games are not intended to tire the horse, but to remind him of your leadership and the training he's experienced. Watching the horse move through his gaits will also tell you whether there's a physical problem such as lameness, or discomfort under the saddle (what the old-timers called a *hump in his back*) that could cause a buck when you mount. Even an old, well-trained horse should be turned 360 degrees in each direction before you climb on.

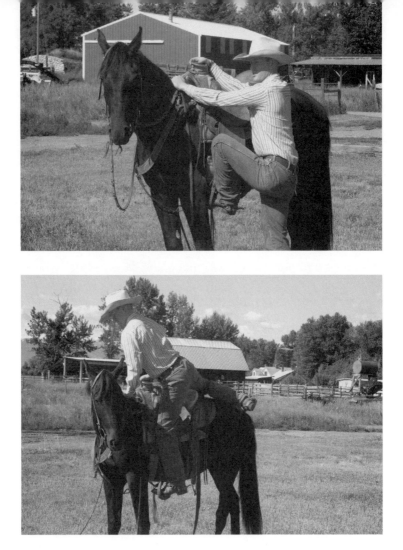

Travis is mounting the best way with left hand on neck and mane, right hand on horn or pommel.

tip 16. Mount the better way

Although mounting on a Western saddle is often done with the left hand on the horn and the right on the cantle (rear) of the saddle, there's a better way. Grasp the reins and a handful of mane with your left hand. Keeping your hand about halfway up the neck, shorten the left rein enough to tip the horse's nose slightly toward you. This way, if the horse moves while you're mounting, he'll tend to move toward you. You can then check him with the rein and a firm "Whoa!"

Next insert your left foot into the stirrup. With your right hand grasp either the horn or the far side of the pommel for additional leverage. In this position your right hand supplies the power, leaving your left hand to manipulate the reins, should that prove necessary. Mounting in this position also keeps your body angled forward, and you'll find the saddle has less tendency to swivel toward you.

Bringing a horse around to one side is your safety valve.

tip 17. Learn the one-rein stop

Checking or stopping a horse by pulling his head around with one rein is among the most fundamental survival techniques. If a horse tries to run away or buck, do not haul back on both reins. That reaction can sometimes do more harm than good by causing the horse to rear or even go over backward, which is potentially deadly. Instead, pull one rein to bend the horse's neck until his nose nearly touches your leg. Horses can rarely buck or run effectively in that position. The instant the horse responds correctly, release the pressure—but be ready to apply it again if necessary.

Of course, the one-rein stop is only effective if the horse has been trained to flex laterally in response to pressure from one rein. A horse that has not had that training is probably not safe to ride.

Emily and Scooter are in light-rein position.

tip 18. Use light rein, not loose rein

Most finished Western horses are trained to proceed with a light rein, just removing the slack as the horse's nose telescopes forward at each step. Although the term *loose rein* is in vogue, reins so loose that they drape in large loops toward the ground should be avoided on the trail. In case of a sudden spook, when a horse must be checked with the one-rein stop, too much rein must be reeled in if there is excessive slack—and much can happen in the interim. In addition, loose flopping reins tend to catch on brush.

tip 19. Avoid being dragged

Among the worst possible scenarios on horseback is falling or being bucked off, getting your foot caught in the stirrup, and then being dragged. We've discussed how proper footwear and the addition of tapaderos can help prevent this horrifying sequence. Breakaway stirrup attachments are also available. If you ever find yourself dragged with your foot caught in a stirrup, try to have the presence of mind to turn over on your belly. In that position, your foot is more likely to come loose.

tip 20. Shape up for safety

One of the best things we can do for safe and comfortable interaction with horses is to improve our physical conditioning. Age tends to weaken our legs and add weight to our torsos. Mounting becomes more difficult. Staying in the saddle during a sudden spook is more challenging as well, because of diminished leg strength and a more top-heavy build. Defenses against this scenario are keeping our weight down and our strength up. Vigorous walking helps the legs, as do deep-knee bends and other exercises. Riding as often as possible keeps you in tune and keeps your balance sharp.

Buddy "helps" Linda catch her horse, but won't go with her on the trail.

tip 21. Leave your dog at home

We all love our dogs. But for safety's sake, there are many good reasons to leave your dog home while you ride the trails. Your horse may be perfectly at ease with your dog darting underfoot on and off the trail. But if your dog runs ahead and meets another party, their horses may not be similarly tolerant—and your dog's sudden appearance could cause a spook for which you'd rather not be responsible. For this reason virtually all organized trail rides prohibit dogs.

Chapter 2

Selecting Your Horse

If you already own the perfect trail or pleasure horse, this section may not seem to apply to you. After all, most of us are pretty stuck on the horses we already own—and if they perform the tasks we require in comfort and safety, we have every right to be satisfied. However, even if you're satisfied with your current horse, the tips in this chapter will prove valuable for the inevitable day when you begin the search for another horse.

tip 22. Choose the right age

An old rule says the younger you are in years of experience with horses, the older the horse should be. While not absolute, there is much truth to this notion. Horses don't mature physically until age six, and, like humans, they continue to learn throughout their lives. Much of training is endless repetition of the correct behavior, not allowing the incorrect, and a mature horse that has been handled properly has training much more deeply ingrained than that of a young horse.

However, an old horse with bad habits may be equally set in behavior of the wrong sort, such as being *barn soured*, a term for the horse that refuses to go out alone. If you're new to horses, try to find a mature horse that is thoroughly trained for the trail. Expect to pay! It's unlikely this horse will be your last one, so as you gain experience, you can consider owning a younger animal. Starting a young horse in training is rewarding but should only come after some years of experience.

tip 23. Pick nice friends

Disposition in horses refers to what we consider personality in humans. We all claim to know what these terms mean, but we have trouble defining them. In the trail horse, we look for an even disposition—a horse that is not quick to spook and take flight, with an attitude that seems friendly to humans but not pushy. (Pushiness is usually the result of humans tolerating the horse getting into their space—nibbling, which becomes nipping, or pawing, which becomes striking; each behavior grows as respect for the human wanes.)

A horse that lays his ears back or bares his teeth—or worse, whirls his hind end toward you, threatening to kick—is dangerous. Either the disposition or the training—or both—is deficient.

tip 24. Choose a gelding or mare

For your trail horse, you'll want either a gelding or a mare. Lacking reproductive cycles, geldings (neutered males) are considered by many people to have a more even day-to-day disposition. Those of us partial to mares will tout their superior drive—the reason the Pony Express used them exclusively. In truth all sorts of gradations occur within the ranks of both geldings and mares, and the choice is a personal one.

Why not a stallion? Stallions are reproductive machines. The best trained can indeed perform tractably in mixed company, but expert handling is required. One never forgets that a stallion is a stallion and is fully capable of acting like one in the blink of an eye. Thus, stallions are barred from many organized trail rides.

tip 25. Look for the best type of horse

Good trail and pleasure horses come from all light-horse breeds, but breeds of the *saddle type*—those developed primarily for smooth, efficient horseback transportation—are particularly suited. The selective breeding of these animals has emphasized endurance and smooth, rapid gaits that are comfortable to the rider. They have not been bred for all-out racing speed, acceleration, or the ability to perform one specialized arena event. Among the many breeds that contain a particularly high percentage of good trail prospects are the Morgan (older style), Tennessee Walking Horse, American Saddlebred, Missouri Foxtrotter, and Peruvian Paso. Regardless of breed, it's wise to choose a horse that comes from *using* stock, from a stable, ranch, or farm that emphasizes backcountry riding rather than arena performance exclusively.

This horse has withers that hold the saddle with little pressure from the cinch.

tip 26. Select high withers

High withers are an extremely important conformation feature in the trail horse. They tend to hold the saddle in place and keep it from slipping from side to side while you mount, so the cinch (girth) need not be so tight. The withers prevent the saddle from slipping forward when you drop steeply downhill, and they also act as a sort of fulcrum to the horse's movement—perhaps the reason that prominent withers tend to be found in horses with a rapid walk.

This stallion, Absaroka Silver Dollar, shows an excellent topline for carrying weight: short back, strong loin, and uphill build.

tip 27. Study the topline

Two other conformation features desirable in trail and backcountry horses are a short back and an *uphill* build. The uphill build—withers higher than the top of the croup—tends to go both with walking ability and a back that holds the saddle well. The short back is necessary for weight-carrying ability. Trail and pleasure horses are often called upon to carry heavier loads and to carry them for longer periods than horses that perform in arena events. On a desirable topline, the withers seem to rise from the middle of the back.

Skywalker's feet have excellent walls, are adequate in size for his weight, and are shod for the trail, with no excess toe.

tip 28. Look for good feet

Old-timers fond of saying "No foot, no horse" were expressing how important good feet are to the soundness of horses. This is particularly true for trail horses that take their riders miles from farriers and veterinarians. Some breeders have made the mistake of developing strains of horses with petite feet that are too small to bear the horse's weight over a lifetime of rugged use. In addition to adequate size, the feet of the trail horse should have thick hoof walls. Farriers are some of the best judges of hooves because they've learned to recognize the sort of feet that give little trouble over the long haul.

Bone measured this way is a good indicator of overall structure.

tip 29. Measure the bone

Equine physiologist Deb Bennett, PhD, has studied the skeletal remains of horses originating from prehistoric times. She decries the loss of bone in domestic horses, the result of breeding for elegance rather than utility. A good indicator of a horse's bone structure can be determined by measuring the circumference of the foreleg just below the knee. You're measuring sinew and skin, of course, not just bone; but as with measuring the wrist size of a human, you get a good comparative snapshot of relative bone mass. Dr. Bennett's requirement is for at least 7 inches of bone for each 1,000 pounds of horse. Interestingly, many heavily built, muscular horses fall short.

tip 30. Consider going gaited

Through the ages humans have bred strains of horses featuring smooth, rapid, four-beat gaits in which each foot hits the ground singly. Gaits such as the amble, running walk, rack, single-foot, and foxtrot replace the two-beat trot, in which the right front and left rear hit simultaneously. Four-beat gaits are normally much smoother than two-beat gaits, so horses able to perform them have been popular in many areas of the world where long distances had to be covered on horseback, including the British Isles, South and Central America, and much of the United States. Teddy Roosevelt wrote of a hunting trip in the Black Hills of South Dakota in 1892:

> My foreman and I rode beside the wagon on our wiry, unkempt, unshod cattle ponies. They carried us all day at a rack, pace, single-foot or slow lope . . .; the trot, the favorite gait with eastern park-riders, is disliked by all peoples who have to do much of their life-work in the saddle.

The arena horse can normally be hauled by trailer to the location where he performs, so smooth gaits are less important. By contrast, the trail rider often rides for the sheer enjoyment of the experience, and over long distances a smooth ride becomes much appreciated.

Thus, gaited breeds such as the Tennessee Walking Horse, Missouri Foxtrotter, Peruvian Paso, Paso Fino, Rocky Mountain Horse, and Icelandic Horse continue to grow in popularity among trail and pleasure riders.

tip 31. Identify weight-carrying capability

The trail horse is often called upon to carry much heavier weights than horses in competitive events. If you're heavy you may assume you need a tall horse, but that isn't necessarily the case. Weight-carrying ability is more allied to conformation and physical conditioning than it is to the horse's own weight or height. A short back is important for carrying heavy loads, as is a broad loin. Between the back of the rib cage and the pelvis, loin muscles lie on each side of the backbone and extend outward and down. Structure of the loin muscles explains why smaller breeds such as the Icelandic and the Pasos have a reputation for great weight-carrying ability compared to their size. Dr. Deb Bennett's booklet series, *Principles of Conformation Analysis*, explains in detail how to measure and evaluate the loin.

Skywalker, at 16.1 (65 inches) is at the upper limits of practical size for a trail horse.

tip 32. Measure in hands

As we've said previously, large size may not be very important—even if you are heavy. Horses bred for riding range from 14.2 hands (measured from the ground to the top of the withers) to 16 hands, with ponies standing under 14.2 and warmbloods, dressage horses, and other sport horses often ranging even taller.

A hand is 4 inches. The second number indicates the additional inches and is not a decimal. Therefore, 15.3 indicates 63 inches. Add another inch, and the horse is 16 hands.

Trail riders often find small to moderate-sized horses more athletic in rough terrain, easier to mount without a block or other assistance, and handier on the trail when you must duck branches and traverse obstacles.

Emily's mare, Doll, is undaunted by the roar of whitewater under the bridge.

tip 33. Identify the finished trail horse

Finished is a common but inaccurate term when applied to horses or humans. Both species learn their entire lives. However, a trail horse sold as finished should not spook in an uncontrolled manner, should cross water and bridges without fuss, and should be comfortable with jackets or slickers flopping around behind the saddle. Such a horse should be accustomed to livestock and wildlife (but allowed a sudden start if a grouse were to fly out between its legs). Further, the *complete* trail horse should neck-rein so that only one hand is required for riding, respond to leg cues, back readily, load into even a two-horse trailer, pony another horse, and not show hostility to other equines while under saddle.

Chapter 3

Training the Trail Horse

You may not fancy yourself a horse trainer, if that description means starting colts from scratch. But if you interact with horses, you're teaching the animal and improving his training in one way or another. Understanding the principles and a few of the techniques is critical.

tip 34. To ride is to train

If you are riding, you are training. Either you are training the horse, or the horse is training you. You either enforce the training the horse already has (and perhaps add to it) or you let it lapse and allow the horse to take charge. Although we all aim for horses that are friends and companions, they must not be our equals—because they have ten times our strength. For safety's sake, we must remain their leaders.

You are not doing the horse a favor if you allow him to throw to the winds the discipline that has been instilled in him by past trainers. Horses that become unmanageable by spoiling tend to come to unfortunate ends. Be kind—but always assertive.

tip 35. Use pressure and release

Pressure and release is the essence of all horse training. It's expressed in different ways by different schools of training, but the explanations all boil down to the same principle: Pressure of some sort is applied. Then, when the correct response occurs, the pressure is released. The release is the horse's reward for doing the correct thing. The art of horse training is being able to choose the technique most effective for applying the pressure, and being precise in timing the release.

tip 36. Stay at it

Be consistent, firm, and patient. Horses are very habitual creatures. See to it that they do the right thing, reward them, and stay at it. If a problem arises, attempt to decipher what's wrong—but keep trying. Hundreds of repetitions of the correct behavior make a trained horse.

tip 37. Train on both sides

Horses have split vision, the eye on one side seeing nearly half of the 360 degrees around them, the other eye seeing the other half, with overlap only toward the front. As mentioned earlier, they have a small blind spot directly in front and directly behind. Horses also seem more "split-brained" than humans. Because you teach your horse to tolerate the slap of a stirrup leather on his near (left) side, don't assume he's gained the same knowledge on the right. Some transference of learning from one side to the other does occur, but it's safest to assume that each learned response must be taught again on the other side.

tip 38. Get the "boogers" out

Patiently accustom your horse to each new touch, sound, and movement. Some trainers use the term *desensitization*, while others dislike that word because it implies you're somehow "dumbing down" the horse. You want all his senses alive, but you don't want him to be afraid of harmless sights, sounds, or smells. Be assertive. If the horse jumps as you place a blanket on his back, don't quit. Try to place it a little more gently, perhaps, but continue until the horse ignores the blanket completely. Then go to the other side and start over. In each case, stay at the task until there's some improvement. If, however, you detect that you've tackled a task for which the horse is not ready, don't be afraid to scale down and accomplish something similar but less challenging before you quit. End each session on a positive note.

Travis has started with the left front and will teach the horse to lead with each foot.

tip 39. Teach your horse to lead by each foot

A horse that readily yields each foot will be a joy to your farrier, will be less likely to hurt himself if caught in wire, and will readily adjust to hobbles or picketing by one front foot. Teach him to lead by each foot in a small round pen if possible. Tie a soft cotton rope around your horse's pastern, starting with his left front. Or, use a hobble half, attaching the snap of a long lead rope to its ring. Don't try to pull the horse anywhere. Instead, just take the slack out of the rope. You'll be surprised at how quickly your horse learns he can create comfortable slack in the rope by moving toward you. Then tighten again. Soon he'll follow you. Then start with another foot. Often you can progress through all four feet in less than an hour.

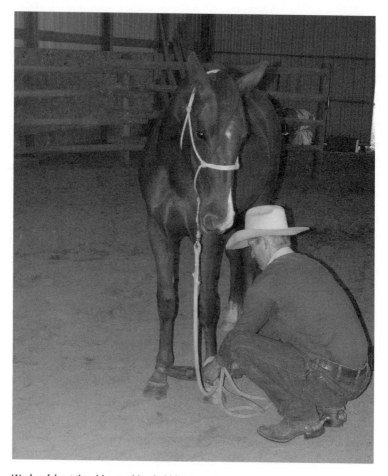

Work safely at the side attaching hobbles to pasterns.

tip 40. Hobble your horse

All trail horses should understand hobbles. Often it's impractical to tie a horse, and tying to trees should be avoided as much as possible. Train your horse on soft ground with padded hobbles. If you've already taught your horse to readily yield each foot for trimming or shoeing, and if you've taught him to lead by each foot, he'll accept hobbles easily. Attach them to the pastern of each front foot, working from the side. Be careful while buckling the second side—lest your horse startles when the job is half done. Tell him "Whoa" during the process; then step off to his side and hold him by a lead rope at first, until he realizes he's restrained.

tip 41. Teach ground driving

Ground driving teaches the basics of control with reins. Start with only a halter, progressing to a snaffle bit as the colt becomes used to it. The long reins can be run through the stirrups of a Western saddle (tie the stirrups together under the horse's belly with a soft rope to keep them from flopping around), but that position is a little low. If your saddle has D-rings that are located higher, they'll work well. Best of all is a surcingle or bitting rig.

Your colt will drive better if he already knows impulsion, whether taught by "natural" horsemanship methods (with long lead rope) or other traditional round pen tools and methods. During ground driving you can teach "Whoa" (which means to stop and stand still until signaled to move), direct reining left and right, and backing. The constant contact with long reins along flanks and rump prepares the colt for riding.

tip 42. Know your bits

The science of bits and bitting is extremely involved, sometimes sparking sharp disagreement between various schools of horse training. However, most horsemanship requires knowledge of only a few basic types of bits.

Because the snaffle has no shanks and provides only direct side pressure with no leverage, it is very popular for starting colts. As with all bits, however, the snaffle can be severe in rough hands.

Curb bits have shanks that provide leverage on the curb strap underneath the horse's chin, on the bars of the mouth (the area without teeth), and, to a degree, on the poll just behind the animal's ears. Location of the fulcrum point, shape of the mouthpiece, length of the shanks, and other factors determine leverage and severity. Use no more leverage than required, but don't be afraid to make a change. As with all devices for training horses—spurs, whips, long lead ropes— greater leverage means you must have lighter hands.

Ponying a colt is good early training.

tip 43. Pony your colt

Ponying (leading from another horse) can accustom a colt to traveling over varied terrain in a controlled manner. The horse you ride must be steady, unflappable, and used to ropes touching him everywhere, even under his tail. Do not tie the colt's lead rope to your saddle in any fashion, and do not wrap it around your hand. The safest method is to simply hold the rope. But as the colt becomes more reliable, you may—if you're using a Western saddle—take one dally (wrap) around the saddle horn, keeping your thumb upward. Do not allow the colt to get in front of you. Shorten the slack in the lead rope if necessary, and slow him down with a series of jerks.

tip 44. Pack your colt

A packsaddle is a wonderful training device. The breeching, which runs under the tail and holds a load from moving forward, teaches the horse to tolerate ropes and straps in strange places. Adding panniers containing relatively light loads, perhaps a sack of feed in each, accustoms the colt to carrying weight. As you pony the colt, the panniers scraping on trees and bouncing a little further desensitizes the animal to strange touches and sounds. The colt that has been successfully packed rarely objects strenuously to his first experience carrying a human.

tip 45. Teach the side pass

The side pass is best taught early while the colt is still direct reining. For a side pass left, face a wall or fence and cue vigorously with your right leg fairly far forward. The colt is used to this signal to turn left, but now you don't let him do so. Instead use your reins to keep him facing the wall. If he's been taught to give to leg pressure, the horse will eventually take a tentative step sideways. Praise him for that. Sometimes it works well to ride at an angle to the wall, then keep his momentum in the same direction, which is now translated to sideways movement. It takes patience with much praise and release of pressure when the colt does the right thing, but in time he'll go sideways by crossing his legs at every step. Out on the trail you'll be able to press him gently to one side or another, to move away from danger, another rider, or an unyielding tree.

Dan starts Pride's early neck-rein training for a right turn with three cues: right direct rein, left neck rein, and left leg.

tip 46. Teach the neck-rein

Neck-reining can be taught from the very first ride. Each time you turn the colt left, give three signals: a direct pull on the left rein, right rein contact on the colt's neck, and a leg cue forward on the horse's right side. For a right turn, do the opposite. Soon the tug in the direction you're turning will be unnecessary, and the colt will neck-rein with help from the leg cue until eventually that cue will also be unnecessary. Your goal is a horse that you can ride with one hand, steering with nothing more than a subtle movement of your rein hand in the direction in which you wish to turn.

Equipment for the Trail Horse

Riding traditions and the equipment involved in the use of horses for both work and sport vary immensely throughout the world. In many cases, these differences are a matter of culture or personal preference rather than right or wrong, wise or unwise. The recommendations that follow, however, are related to safety and others to comfort.

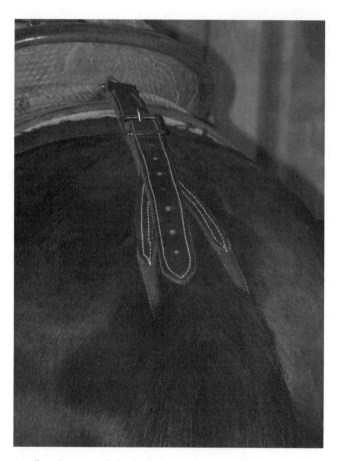

A well-made crupper helps the horse on steep descents.

tip 47. Use a crupper

A crupper helps the horse hold the saddle in place on steep down-hill grades. Particularly needed on low-withered horses, the crupper is helpful for all. A horse's tail contains a large bone with strong muscles, and he'll quickly learn to clamp the tail onto the crupper when he heads down steep slopes. Do give the horse some time, perhaps saddled and turned loose in a round pen or corral, to get used to the feel of a new object under his tail.

Extensive riding on trails blasted from granite requires proper shoeing.

tip 48. Shoe as needed

Traditional shoeing consists of nailing an iron horseshoe to the rim of a horse's hoof. No pain is involved, because the nail penetrates hoof material corresponding to the portion of your fingernail that you regularly trim. Many substitutes for traditional shoes have appeared, and time will tell whether they're as effective. Some people believe in leaving horses barefoot, allowing the hoof to toughen. This will happen to a degree, but don't count on it for adequate protection over extremely rocky terrain. All horses are domestic animals, not wild, and selective breeding has not always retained the thick hoof walls and large feet of their ancestors. Further, before domestication, horses evolved on grassy plains, not in stony mountains or on cobbled streets or pavement. Prehistoric horses weren't called upon to carry riders, pull wagons, or compete in speed events.

With a tackaberry you don't need to thread the latigo each time you saddle. The tongue on this cinch could be removed, since it's no longer used.

tip 49. Try a tackaberry

The tackaberry is a handy device for Western saddles, loved by early cowboys but not common in tack shops today. Basically, it's a hook that snags the cinch ring and holds it securely. You saddle and unsaddle by attaching and detaching this hook, which avoids the necessity of threading the latigo each time.

tip 50. Take two first aid kits

It's a given that a small first aid kit for humans is required equipment on the trail. But for longer trips far from help, one member of the party should also carry an extensive equine first aid kit. Ask your veterinarian for assistance in assembling such a kit.

Some suggested items include: bandage material, such as sheet cotton, rolled gauze, and Vetrap; disinfectant, such as Nolvasan; antibiotics (ask your vet for recommendations here); anti-inflammation medication, such as "bute" and Banamine; a pair of hemostats; a tongue depressor; and nitrofurazone wound dressing.

tip 51. Keep saddlebags small

The worst possible location on a horse's back for carrying weight is be-hind the saddle, over the kidneys. The problem with large saddlebags and the saddle packs designed to carry overnight camping gear is that they tempt you to fill them with unneeded items, to the possible detri-ment of the horse. Keep your saddlebags small and light. If you must carry heavier items such as water bottles or backpacking stoves, select pommel or horn packs that fit on the front of the saddle.

Cell phones are good safety devices, but don't ruin a ride with unnecessary use of them.

tip 52. Take a cell phone

Recommending cell phones as trail riding equipment is painful, given their level of obnoxious overuse. No one goes on a trail ride to hear another person's phone conversation; we have enough of that in restaurants and airports. Further, a call back to the office just might ruin the magic of the aspen grove where you dismount for lunch and drown out the babbling of the nearby brook. Since horses often spook at incongruous noises, a cell phone that rings while you traverse a ledge trail might spell disaster.

However, the cell phone can be used to call for life-saving assistance in an emergency. Take one along on trail rides, but leave it turned off and tucked away in a saddlebag, agreeing with others to use it only in case of an emergency. Then remember its limitations. Often cell phones will not work in deep canyons because "line of sight" to their cell towers is required.

Chapter 5

Coping with Spooks

Nothing intimidates pleasure riders more than the tendency of horses to suddenly react to something real or imaginary that frightens them. Spooking results in more injuries to riders than bucking, yet all horses do spook periodically. Here are some reasons why horses behave that way and some suggestions for coping.

tip 53. Understand why they spook

Your horse spooks because to spook, throughout his evolution, has been to survive. The ability to come from a rest position (grazing head down in a pasture) to full flight (galloping away from what frightens him) is deep in the horse's psyche. His primary reaction to the unknown has always been to run away. Domestication has not removed the escape reaction—and some vestiges will remain no matter how thorough the training. Don't refer to any horse as spookproof, childproof, or bombproof.

tip 54. Be ready

Because spooking is in a horse's nature, riding is active, never passive. You must never simply sit on a horse as you would on a park bench. Readiness is everything. Adopt a posture of readied relaxation. Expect the unexpected. Even the best-trained horse is likely to react suddenly to the appearance of a bear on the trail, a pheasant clattering into the air, or a hiker's dog bursting from the brush.

tip 55. Recognize three kinds of spooks

There are good spooks, bad spooks, and fake spooks. A good spook is a slight jerk or start that runs through the horse's body but is immediately brought under control by the horse's training. A bad spook is uncontrolled—the horse bolts, bucks, or rears. When a fake spook occurs, the horse is putting you on. He's really not frightened, but thinks he can get out of something such as crossing an obstacle by allowing it to scare him. Endurance riders note that heart and respiratory rates don't spike during fake spooks.

Only good spooks are acceptable. Bad spooks indicate a need for more training. Your defense is the one-rein stop (see tip 17). Fake spooks indicate a need for assertive riding. The fake spook is a horse's attempt to pull something on the rider, to get out of an unpleasant situation by feigning fright. The assertive rider will use his legs and perhaps his voice to spell out that he or she, not the horse, is in control.

Chapter 6

Correcting Problems

Few people have relationships with horses that are totally trouble free. As with human relations, there are occasional bumps in the trail. Getting past them is usually a matter of clear thinking, understanding, and discipline. Some problems, however, are dangerous and better left to professionals.

tip 56. Correct the barn sour horse

The term *barn sour* refers to horses that don't wish to leave the home place or wherever their buddies are located. Barn sour horses are normally bluffers. They proceed down the trail for a distance and then attempt to turn around and go home. Sometimes the attempt is a gentle one, and an assertive rider diffuses it by applying leg pressure or perhaps a slap on the rump. However, the same horse may treat a timid rider differently by acting more worried and determined to turn around. If he succeeds, the horse has successfully begun training the rider, and he'll be all the more difficult next time.

The best treatment for the barn sour horse is vigorous impulsion to nip in the bud his first attempts to turn around. A truly spoiled horse, one that attempts to rear or buck if he doesn't get his way, can be dangerous and is best corrected by a professional.

tip 57. Motivate the laggard

The laggard, even though physically sound and capable, saunters up the trail and allows a great gap to open between you and the horse in front of you. He may attempt to stop and crop bites of grass along the way. Constant use of your heels won't correct the laggard because he's used to such prompting (probably applied timidly by inexperienced riders) and ignores it.

First, check with your vet to make sure the horse is not hampered physically but is simply taking advantage of you. That determined, it will probably take a good whack on his rear to get the horse motivated. The important thing is to give a good decisive stimulus, but follow it by release the moment he speeds up. Constant, nagging pressure (kicking the horse at every step) has not done the job. The horse must be rewarded for doing the correct thing. If you don't feel capable of handling the possible reaction to assertive stimulus, have a professional begin this correction for you.

tip 58. Cool the charger

The charger has the same problem as the laggard, but because his personality is different, the problem takes a different form. He too has been handled with steady pressure and no release: riders have hauled back on the reins whenever they're on him, or perhaps have used a succession of increasingly severe bits. The horse has learned to handle the bit pressure and do as he pleases—which is to charge up the trail faster than you want him to go, and perhaps insist on being in the lead.

First try coping with a vigorous jerk back on the reins. He'll slow momentarily and you'll reward him—even if only for an instant—with a slackening of rein pressure. Continue this way. The horse may begin to recognize that there's a reward (freedom from rein tension) when he responds to your yank on the reins. (You won't likely hurt the horse's mouth; the charger is far beyond that.) An extreme case may take retraining in the round pen, perhaps with a snaffle bit, teaching the horse to come around laterally as he should have been taught in the first place. Such a horse can then be spun in circles if he refuses to slow down.

tip 59. Survive a runaway

If you ever experience a runaway, do your best to pull the horse around with the one-rein stop (see tip 17). If the horse has gained speed, don't haul back all at once. Try to bring the horse into a circular course, gradually tightening the circle. If you can't do that, you may be able to head the horse up a hill formidable enough to slow him down. If his headlong rush is toward other horses, it's likely that your horse is attempting to return to the herd—and he's likely to slow or stop when he reaches the others. A horse with a penchant for attempting to run away needs professional attention.

tip 60. Handle a buck

If a horse attempts to buck, keep his head up and pull it around, just as you would were he trying to run away. A true bucker needs retraining, but the colt that bucks once or twice can usually be controlled by pulling around in this way. The instant the animal stops this antisocial behavior, slacken the rein as reward, but be ready. He may not be over it, and he may use the slack for a second attempt at bucking you off.

tip 61. Deal with rearing

Rearing is extremely dangerous because it can lead to going over backward. Never train a horse to rear—leave that to Hollywood stunt people. The best cure for getting "light in front" is impulsion forward. Horses rear in an attempt to escape: perhaps you're not allowing the horse to go forward, or the horse is refusing to go forward so he goes upward instead. Impel such a horse forward in no uncertain terms, or, if you can't go forward, spin him around. Do *not* haul back on both reins—you may pull the horse over backward on top of you.

tip 62. If you survive a horse going over backward . . .

Going over backward is the most dangerous thing a horse can do. If it should ever happen, try very hard to push your body off to one side, completely dismounting if possible, as the accident develops. If you survive, *never ride that horse again*! Do not believe for an instant that even a professional can correct the problem. Take a loss on the horse, selling it loose through a sale as unsafe to ride, or have a veterinarian put it down. Yes, these actions are extreme. But so is the action that nearly got you killed, and there is no 100 percent guarantee that it won't happen again.

Chapter 7

Backcountry Riding

Riding in rough country is too little taught. Eventing, foxhunting, and other activities teach demanding skills and require fast riding over hill and dale—but they emphasize things quite different from riding a ledge trail above a cliff in the Rocky Mountains, leading a pack string, or coping with wild animals on the trail. Here are some tips for handling rough country challenges.

tip 63. Go straight up and straight down

Steep, short banks, perhaps 10 or 15 feet tall, such as barrow ditches on the sides of highways, should be handled by riding straight up or straight down. On bad footing, the horse going straight down can normally slide safely for this short distance, if he loses his footing. Going up, he will normally scramble his way to the top. However, if you traverse this steep slope at an angle, the horse's four feet can slip out from under him, causing his body to fall uphill and pin your leg beneath it.

These riders are properly resisting the temptation to lean back on a steep descent.

tip 64. Handle hills

Riding steeply uphill requires you to lean forward to keep your weight as close as possible over the horse's center of gravity. That is normally located just behind the foreleg and about one-third of the way up a horse's body. (The actual center varies considerably from horse to horse.)

Conventional wisdom suggests that if you lean forward going uphill you should lean backward going downhill, but riding academies teach students to lean forward even going downhill, particularly at speed. Why? Leaning backward downhill tends to hamper a horse's ability to get his hind legs up under his body, which is essential for the horse's ability to descend steep slopes safely. Since leaning back can cause a horse to fall, a good compromise for the trail rider who normally descends at slower speeds is to sit upright in the saddle and consciously avoid leaning back.

Both uphill and downhill riding require giving the horse a little more rein. The additional slack gives your horse freedom to lunge up a slope and to brace his legs under him going down.

Emily looks straight at the point where she wishes to emerge from the stream, helping Scooter stay on track.

tip 65. Cross streams safely

Streams come in many sizes and types, from slow and muddy to swift and clear. Here are some general guidelines:

- Slow waters often do run deep. Beware of little-used crossings with slow, muddy water that doesn't allow you to see the bottom.

- Shallow, clear crossings over rocky bottoms—even if the water is swift—are usually safe, assuming your horse is properly shod. Swift water that touches a horse's belly, however, may be more than he can handle.

- Where heavily traveled horse trails cross streams, the ford is normally safe unless recent storms or spring runoff are causing high water.

- Because cattle cross at a particular place, don't assume the crossing is safe for horses. Cattle, because of their easygoing dispositions and cloven hooves, can cross boggy areas that might trap a horse.

- While crossing, fix your vision on the point toward which you wish to head. To look down at the water can cause imbalance in the horse and vertigo in the rider. If the water is swift, angle upstream.

- Should your horse lose his footing and fall, or reach water deeper than you'd estimated and begin swimming, kick clear of the horse and try to stay upstream of him. You don't want the horse's body to trap you against a rock or log.

tip 66. Face the edge while turning around

If you must turn around on a ledge trail, turn the horse toward the drop-off edge so he faces the danger. He'll keep his front legs on the trail. If you put his rear end toward the edge, he's less skillful at knowing his limits and may place a foot over the side. If the trail is extremely narrow and treacherous, get off and lead him around—but do so in the same direction, with his head toward the drop-off.

tip 67. Tie with a halter rope, not the reins

Reins are for riding; lead ropes are for tying. The most comfortable reins for riding the finished horse are slim leather; but if a horse is tied with them and pulls back, the reins can break. Thus the horse might "train himself" to pull back. Further, the horse may hurt his mouth by jerking against the bit in the process. Instead, tie him with a lead rope attached to a halter. For trail riding, it's easiest to merely leave the halter under the bridle while you ride, particularly if it's the flat type, which will cause the horse no discomfort.

tip 68. Watch for wildlife

Nearly anywhere you ride, you're likely to encounter some sort of wildlife. Even park squirrels, rabbits, and birds that flush from beneath your horse's feet can cause spooks. Whitetail deer seem to live nearly everywhere. The more opportunity your horse has to graze in large pastures outside stalls and barns, the more likely he'll be used to some of the more common critters—but you must always be ready. What he accepts as natural in his home pasture still might scare him on the trail.

Only a few species of wildlife actually pose any sort of danger. Moose can be aggressive, particularly during mating season or if protecting their young. Black bears (which actually come in many colors from black to brown to yellow) are normally afraid of humans and can usually be bluffed off the trail. The grizzly is another story, but is found only in a few areas of the United States, so an encounter is unlikely. Mountain lions (also called cougars and pumas) are on the increase across most of the United States and can be dangerous to humans, particularly if you turn and run from them.

If you're mounted on a horse, chances of an attack by any of these animals is very slight. Injury because of your horse's violent reaction to a predatory presence is far more likely; keep the lid on using the one-rein stop if necessary, then evacuate the area in as controlled a fashion as possible. Again, chances of any trouble are miniscule. Truth be known, I'd rather encounter a black bear on the trail than have my horse step on a skunk before I spotted it.

tip 69. Cope with cattle

In many areas of the United States you'll encounter cattle on the trail, particularly on forest service or BLM (Bureau of Land Management) acres that lease grazing rights. Riders with rural roots are likely to pass through cattle with scarcely a glance, but urbanites are often intimidated. Normally there's no worry. Cattle are domestic animals and are accustomed to being moved by humans (often on horseback). Riding toward them with some whistling or a loud admonition to move will normally pressure them out of your way. It's wise to get your horse used to them in advance, however. One of the best ways is to find a farmer or rancher who will pasture your horse for a few days in or around cows. Any fear will soon be gone.

Cattle, however, are less a flight animal than horses are, and cows will often aggressively defend their calves. Bulls are rarely aggressive to someone on horseback, but do watch for signs of fight typical of bovines: shaking the head, pawing the ground, and mooing in a low, drawn-out, threatening fashion.

Chapter 8

Handling Obstacles

Nearly every trained saddle horse will progress smoothly down a groomed trail, but most riders eventually venture beyond bridle paths in city parks. Streams, logs across the trail, harmless objects that horses misunderstand and thus fear: they all require much learning for the green horse and an occasional refresher for the finished one. Since most horses will occasionally try to balk at something that scares them, here are suggestions for handling the horse's fear and for safely traversing such bumps along the road.

tip 70. Try the low-stress approach

Although there are times when a horse simply needs prodding to go through or past something that scares him (see tip 55), more often than not the fear is real. Horses see anything new as threatening. Should a horse balk at an object that looks strange to him, such as a big boulder or a reflective sign by the side of the trail, first move the horse to the side, if possible, so that he views the object from a slightly different angle. If that's not enough to make him recognize the object as harmless, just back him up a step and keep him looking at the object until you feel him relax. Then move him toward it until he stiffens. Then let him relax again. Repeat the process. Your aim is not simply to drive him past the object but to let him discover for himself that it's harmless. This can take time, but the result is worth it. The same approach can be used to handle fear of the obstacles discussed hereafter.

If your horse hesitates to enter the water, keep him looking at the place you want to go.

tip 71. Accustom your horse to water

Earlier we discussed crossing streams safely (see tip 65). Balking at water crossings is a common problem for horses that are new to the trail. Use the low-stress approach described previously, keeping the horse looking at the place where you'd like him to cross. Small streams are often more difficult than wider streams, which horses seem better able to visualize and understand. Take your time, and be patient and firm—even stubborn if necessary. Keep the horse looking at the water, and eventually he'll step into it.

Practice at home for logs you'll encounter later on the trail.

tip 72. Cross logs on the trail

In a best-case scenario, downed trees across the trail will be sawn and removed using the saw you should carry and the muscle power your party is willing to contribute to improve the trail for all. (A type of saw known as the Oregon Pruning Saw, which cuts only on the pull stroke, is especially effective and safe.) Should the situation or the size of the logs make clearing impossible, your horse will have to step over them or jump, unless there's an easy detour around. Emphasize quietly stepping over the log, rather than jumping it, reining your horse back slightly as you start over to discourage jumping. (Jumping is fun, but footing on the far side may make for questionable landing.) First remove any protruding branches that may endanger the horse's belly. Prepare for this sort of obstacle at home by stepping your horse over poles, then progressing to larger objects such as hay bales.

Chapter 9

Trailering

Trailering horses, because it so tightly confines such powerful animals, can be dangerous. Here are some tips for staying safe.

Emily sends Scooter into the trailer rather than leading him into its confines.

tip 73. Drive, don't lead

Avoid being trapped in front of a horse in a trailer. To this end, teach your horse to load by being driven, rather than led. Techniques using the long lead rope for impulsion are one approach to this end. Driving the horse forward with the lead rope between your body and an arena wall is good preparation.

Scooter backs out, even from larger trailers that would allow room to turn around.

tip 74. Back him out

Similarly, horses should be taught to back out of trailers rather than turning around inside, even if the trailer is large. If you must turn the horse around, be well behind it with a long lead rope, cueing it around. Don't allow yourself to be pinned against the trailer wall as the horse turns around.

Chapter 10

Carrying Your Gear

The foxhunter or three-day eventer rides with just his body and a light saddle, but the trail rider often carries a considerable amount of gear. If he or she is a hunter, birder, fisherman, photographer, or camper with enough equipment to stay overnight, carrying gear without injury to the horse becomes paramount.

tip 75. Cut the weight

Commercial riding concessions often limit loads on horses or mules based on a percentage of the animal's own weight. For some the limit is 20 percent, while others use 25 percent (as did the early U.S. Cavalry). Actually, weight-carrying ability has much more to do with the conformation and physical conditioning of the horse than with its size, as discussed earlier (see tip 31).

One thing is clear, however: if we can lighten the load whenever possible, our horses will perform better and be more comfortable. Add the weight of an average American wearing riding attire and boots to that of a Western saddle, halter, bridle, lead rope, and light saddle bags containing a minimum of equipment (lunch, first aid kit, and rain slicker) and the total weight mounts alarmingly. Choose light gear whenever you can, but don't sacrifice saddle fit and quality to save a few pounds. Try to cut the weight of everything your horse carries, including yourself—most of us can stand to lose a few pounds.

Keep heavy items such as water bottles up front. Horn packs are useful for heavy, angular items.

tip 76. Distribute weight properly

Even more important than the total amount carried by the horse is the distribution of weight on the horse's back. It's essential that the weight be forward, near the horse's natural center of gravity (see tip 64). Too much weight behind the cantle of the saddle can damage a horse's kidneys. This is the main problem with single-horse packing systems and huge saddlebags that encourage overfilling. Keep only very light items behind a horse's saddle. Heavier things, such as water bottles and binoculars, belong forward in horn (pommel) packs. For overnight camping trips with more than the absolute minimum of gear, learn packing skills so that you can properly utilize a packhorse or mule.

Elastic harnesses are available to hold your camera or binoculars in place while you ride.

tip 77. Harness your camera or binoculars

Today's tiny digital cameras can ride in a shirt or jacket pocket. For larger cameras or binoculars, try an elastic harness that keeps the device tucked securely against your chest yet easy to raise to eye level. Using this system, instead of a neck strap, the equipment is less likely to bang on the saddle horn each time you mount.

A good location for a saddle scabbard.

tip 78. Pack a rifle correctly

If you're a hunter, you probably already have a strong opinion on the proper use of a saddle scabbard for carrying a big game rifle. Here's mine: the rifle should be slung scope up, butt forward, bolt away from the horse, with the muzzle hanging fairly steeply down (at least 45 degrees) so the rifle is not carried directly under your knee. The scabbard should lie under, not through, the stirrup leathers.

Chapter 11

Finding Your Way

As riders renew their interest in taking their horses into remote backcountry, basic survival skills become more important. One of the most essential is knowing your location at all times.

Essential tools for knowing where you are: map, compass, and GPS.

tip 78. Review land navigation

Traditional land navigation skills using two basic tools, the map and compass, are essential for the backcountry. They are not replaced by GPS. If you never learned how to read a topographical map, orient it with your compass, and apply what it tells you about direction and the lay of the land to the scene in front of you as you ride up the trail, now is the time. Take a course, read materials, and—if necessary—tap an old ex-military friend. The knowledge comes easily, and the security you'll find in the backcountry that comes from knowing where you are at all times will make the experience more enjoyable.

tip 80. Learn to use GPS

GPS, which stands for global positioning system, is a wonderful modern development, easily applied to backcountry horse travel. A small GPS unit, which costs around $100, is a tremendous supplement to your map and compass. The unit reads your position by locking onto radio transmissions from several satellites. It can tell you your exact position, the direction to a waypoint you've entered earlier, speed, distance traveled, time, altitude, and more. Few knowledgeable backcountry horsemen venture into the wilderness these days without GPS, and the units are extremely helpful—even close to home. One limitation is the unit's requirement for direct line of sight to several satellites, which means they sometimes won't work in deep canyons or under a heavy tree canopy. However, battery failure is the major problem, so be sure to take spares.

Chapter 12

Treading Lightly

In a world with a rapidly expanding population, room to ride shrinks daily. Our remaining backcountry is precious, and our presence there, and that of our horses, has potential for impact and damage. Treating the land gently is an imperative. We must leave only tracks, and as few of them as possible.

tip 81. Know the rules

The first step in being a good backcountry citizen is to obey the rules and regulations that exist to protect the land. Because these vary greatly, inquire locally. One national or state forest may have different rules from another nearby, so locate the forest headquarters (easy to do on the Internet) and get the necessary information. Trailheads often post the latest on fire and other travel regulations, so take time to read the bulletins before departing. Safety, too, is involved, such as when fire danger is high. You'll also want to know about a washed-out bridge or mudslide that could block your passage to the mountain lake you plan to fish.

tip 82. Pack it in, pack it out

Virtually all backcountry areas now operate on the "pack it in, pack it out" principle. There are no trash cans, even at trailheads. You are responsible for all the trash you generate, and never so much as a gum wrapper should fall on the trail. Stuff small items of refuse in your pockets along the way, and take trash bags even on day trips.

Further, take time to pick up junk left by others. The cleaner the trail, the less likely it is that someone of marginal conscience will mess things up.

Hitting the trail with a Decker packsaddle and mantied loads.

tip 83. Limit your pack stock

On full-fledged pack trips, avoid taking more animals than absolutely necessary. Don't overload your animals, but load them fully, trying to keep the ratio no greater than one packhorse for two riders. If you use light equipment designed for backpacking, you may be able to get by with one packhorse for three riders. The fewer the animals, the lower the impact.

tip 84. Don't tramp in mud time

If possible, avoid traveling when it's muddy. The wetter the trail, the more likely your horse's hoofprints will become permanent. Horses are big, heavy animals that exert considerable pressure wherever they step. Wet trails are more vulnerable.

tip 85. Don't cut switchbacks

Forest service trails were built to grade specifications so the slope is gentle enough to be handled by horses and pack stock without frequent rests. Switchbacks have been built that zigzag up mountainsides while staying on grade. Stay on the trail! Shortcutting switchbacks is not only dangerous, it causes erosion. Soon another rider takes the same shortcut, and after a few additional riders do so, an illegal trail—which is not on grade—is created. When water runs down the secondary trail, there's soon a gully.

tip 86. Keep your horses back from the shore

Keep livestock 200 feet from water. It's tempting to park your horse right on the shore of a pristine mountain lake while a friend takes your picture, but your horse is likely to drop manure at that point, and suddenly the lake shore is less pristine.

tip 87. Don't abuse trees

Avoid tying to trees. During a brief stop, or when you have to adjust a pack, tying to trees is often inevitable—but keep it to a minimum. Bark can be easily damaged by the lead rope, but more serious impact happens when a horse paws and cups out an area at the base of the tree and damages the roots. Hobbling the horse while tied will minimize this problem.

tip 88. Leave smaller campsites for backpackers

Some campsites are ideally suited to horse packers, but others are ideally suited to backpackers. Leave the smaller sites for hikers. Two backpackers can perch their small tent on a tiny grassy knoll overlooking a lake, and while that spot may tempt you, you'll help build better relations with other trail users if you leave it for those to whom it's best suited.

tip 89. Hobble in camp

Holding horses in camp must also be done in a way that's both secure and of minimum impact. Hobbling (see tip 40) allows the horse to graze and tends to prevent overuse of one area. However, hobbling is permissible only where grazing is allowed.

Don't hobble all your horses. They can travel surprisingly fast while hobbled, and you might just lose the whole bunch when they decide they're tired of the trip and would just as soon go home. Tie one dominant animal that, in a worst-case scenario, could be used to retrieve the others.

tip 90. Build a highline

Since at least some of your horses must be tied securely in camp, build a highline. Choose if possible a higher, rocky area that will tend to be less damaged by horses' hooves. Commercial "tree-savers" or cinches from the packsaddles around the girth of each tree will minimize damage to the bark. (Be sure to brush the cinches before using them on horses again, so that any bits of bark are removed.) Stretch tightly. Either learn a simple knot called the picket-line loop or purchase a piece of hardware called the knot eliminator to allow tying lead ropes to the highline. These allow tying by furnishing a loop through which you can tie. If you're in camp for several days, move the highline to minimize damage to the ground beneath it. When you break camp, scatter the manure underneath and repair damage to the ground with your camp shovel.

Picketing with a hobble half by a front pastern is safest as long as the horse has first been taught to hobble.

tip 91. Picket when you can

Picketing is another method for holding horses in camp. Picket from a front pastern with a hobble half, not from the halter. Make sure there's a swivel somewhere in the picket line, so the rope doesn't become hopelessly twisted and ruined. The best attachment on the other end is to a picket pin with a built-in swivel. Drive the pin securely into the ground.

Picketing is only allowed where grazing is legal. Make sure you move the picket pin frequently to prevent the horse from grazing an unsightly circle.

tip 92. Leave weeds behind

Noxious weeds, native to other areas and imported into the backcountry, are a terrible blight on the environment. Most national forests now require that you bring only weed-free hay or pellets into the backcountry. To help safeguard the environment and cut chances your horse will colic on new feed, switch him several days before departing on your trip. Doing so will prevent weed seeds from being expelled in his manure and defeating your effort to be conscientious.

tip 93. Scatter manure

When leaving your campsite, concentrate on leaving as little evidence as possible that you were ever there. That includes scattering the manure from your horses. (It's fine fertilizer if spread, but an unsightly fly-drawing mess if you leave it in piles.) You should also studiously avoid allowing horses in the actual living area, near tent and kitchen, of your camp.

tip 94. Build campfires correctly

The building of campfires (if allowed) must follow the regulations of the particular agency or private landowner who manages the land you're using. In some areas the fire-pit method is preferred: remove sod in a small circle, dig a shallow pit, and then, when you break camp, scatter ashes and replace the sod. However, more jurisdictions now prefer you to build your fire in the existing fire pit often present at heavily used campsites. Avoid ringing your fire with rocks—once blackened and unsightly, they stay that way. Do not attempt to burn foil, cans, or anything else that isn't completely combustible.

tip 95. Don't cut trees or shrubs

The days of sleeping on a bed of pine boughs are long gone. In most areas, you're not allowed to cut trees or shrubs. Even cutting a dead or downed tree for firewood may not be legal. Inquire first.

tip 96. Properly dispose of human waste

For short stays in the backcountry, the "cat hole" method is recommended. Dig a one shovel-blade deep hole on high ground and away from water; leave the waste inside with toilet paper only; then replace the sod. For longer stays, dig a latrine. Check with the forest or agency for any particular requirements.

tip 97. Keep the bears away

Keep all food outside your tent and downwind from it. Many wilderness areas now require bear-proof food containers, which must be used unless you're willing to stay in camp at all times or go to the trouble of hanging food high from a rope between trees.

tip 98. Stay clean

Use only biodegradable soap for cleaning both your body and your dishes in the backcountry. Avoid perfumes and other scented cosmetics. They've been known to attract bears. Really!

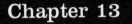

Chapter 13

Where to Go

So your horse is ready, your gear collected, and your trailer serviced. Adventure lies around the next bend. Locate a trail, load up, and go!

tip 99. Find trails public and private

Trail riders in the United States are quite fortunate to live in a country where so much government and private land is open to riders. These acres, however, shrink daily—as development gobbles up open space and other users seek to shut horses out of the backcountry and off the trails. The U.S. Forest Service, the Bureau of Land Management, and numerous state forests allow trail riding on many of their holdings. Additionally, some private landowners, such as major timber companies, allow access. The wonders of the Internet can bring you information on likely locations with the touch of a button.

For those who enjoy riding in much company, many private concessions offer organized trail rides, often with food and campfire entertainment. The advertising sections of magazines such as *The Trail Rider* yield many possibilities.

tip 100. Safeguard your opportunities to ride

Threats to reduce trail riding opportunities can best be handled in two ways. First, be as fine a backcountry citizen as possible. Do everything you can to reduce your impact and to keep the environment clean. Second, join an advocacy group. I particularly recommend Back Country Horsemen of America (www.backcountryhorse.com). BCHA has chapters in many states and several Canadian provinces. Members volunteer to help the forest service with trail improvement projects, and they stay politically active to oppose regulations against horse use in the backcountry.

Above all, have fun!

tip 101. Have fun

A character in *Lonesome Dove* remarks how fine it is to ride "a good horse in new country." Don't let a ringing cell phone or a blaring radio dampen your experience. Leave the office behind. Let the soft footfalls of a good horse take you to the sunshine of a forest clearing and the music of a clear mountain stream. Happy trails!

About the Author

Dan Aadland, with his wife Emily, raises cattle and mountain bred Tennessee Walking Horses on their ranch in south-central Montana. A veteran of many pack trips to the Absaroka Mountains, Aadland emphasizes practical horsemanship in clinics offered at the ranch. In addition to frequent contributions to *Equus*, *The Trail Rider*, and other national magazines, Aadland has written five previous books including *Sketches from the Ranch: A Montana Memoir* and *The Complete Trail Horse*. His Web site is http://my.montana.net/draa.